W9-BMY-805

3 1486 00274 9319

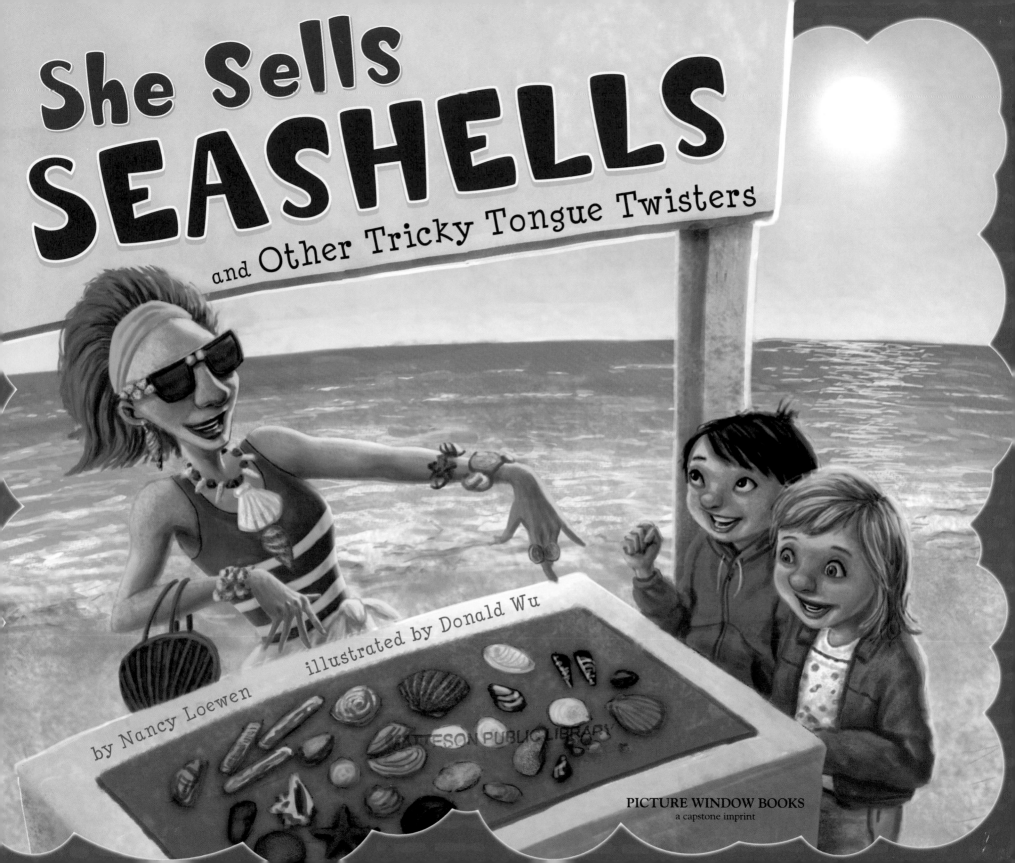

She Sells SEASHELLS
and Other Tricky Tongue Twisters

by Nancy Loewen

illustrated by Donald Wu

PICTURE WINDOW BOOKS
a capstone imprint

MATTESON PUBLIC LIBRARY

What is a tongue twister?

Editor: Jill Kalz
Designer: Lori Bye
Art Director: Nathan Gassman
Production Specialist: Sarah Bennett
The illustrations in this book were created with
water color, pen, and ink.

Picture Window Books
151 Good Counsel Drive
P.O. Box 669
Mankato, MN 56002-0669
877-845-8392
www.capstonepub.com

Copyright © 2011 by Picture Window Books, a Capstone imprint.
All rights reserved. No part of this book may be reproduced without
written permission from the publisher. The publisher takes no responsibility
for the use of any of the materials or methods described in this book, nor for
the products thereof.

All books published by Picture Window Books are manufactured
with paper containing at least 10 percent post-consumer waste.

Library of Congress Cataloging-in-Publication Data
Loewen, Nancy, 1964-
  She sells seashells and other tricky tongue twisters / by Nancy Loewen ;
illustrated by Donald Wu.
      p. cm. – (Ways to say it)
  Includes index.
  ISBN 978-1-4048-6273-9 (library binding)
  ISBN 978-1-4048-6714-7 (paperback)
 1. Tongue twisters–Juvenile literature. 2. English language–Pronunciation.
3. Vocabulary. I. Wu, Donald, ill. II. Title.
PN6371.5.L54 2011
  428.1–dc22   2010033761

Printed in the United States of America in North Mankato, Minnesota.
092010   005933CGS11

*Special thanks to our adviser, Terry Flaherty, PhD,
Professor of English, Minnesota State University, Mankato,
for his expertise.*

A tongue twister **can can as many cans as a canner can can**.

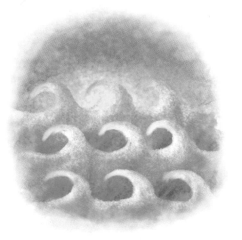

It **goes to sea to see what it can see.**

It might even roll along with

rubber baby buggy bumpers.

When we talk, our brain, tongue, and lips have to work together in the right way. Most of the time, it just happens. But every so often, there's a glitch. The wrong sounds come out. Our tongues "twist."

Tongue twisters make our tongues twist on purpose. They're a challenge for our tongue, brain, and everything in between!

Meet Ken Chen.

Ken is about to have a very strange day.

It all starts when he sees

six sleek swans swimming swiftly southward.

Tongue twisters are fun, but they can be useful too. People who are learning English as a second language often practice tongue twisters to improve their skills.

Tongue twisters make use of alliteration. Alliteration happens when words in a row start with the same letter or letter sound. This tongue twister has six *s*'s in a row. It also has three *sw*'s.

Ken follows his nose to the kitchen.

His mom is talking with their chatty neighbor, Ida.

"And speaking of pancakes," Ida says,

"Betty Botter bought some butter but she said, 'The butter's bitter. If I put it in my batter it will make my batter bitter.' So, she bought some better butter, better than the bitter butter, and she put it in her batter, and her batter was not bitter."

The main words in this tongue twister (*butter, bitter, batter, better*) start with the same letter sound. They end with the same letter sound too.

As he walks to school, Ken sees Mr. Gilbert working on a string of lights. Mr. Gilbert is talking to himself.

"Red bulb, blue bulb, red bulb, blue bulb, red bulb, blue bulb."

Tongue twisters come in all languages—even sign language! Groups of words that are difficult to sign are called "finger fumblers."

This tongue twister has only three words, but it's tough! The *bl* sound at the beginning of *blue* is combined with its opposite, the *lb* sound, at the end of *bulb*.

The surprise quiz at school is truly surprising.
Ken answers as best he can.

How much wood would a woodchuck chuck
if a woodchuck could chuck wood?

A woodchuck would chuck as
much wood as he could chuck if
a woodchuck could chuck wood!

If Stu chews shoes, should Stu choose
the shoes he chews?

Yes. Of course! Who else
would want them?

11

After the quiz, three parents talk to Ken's class about their jobs.
JJ's mom is a salesperson.

She sells seashells by the seashore.

There's a lot of tongue twisting going on in this short phrase. The *sh* sound is repeated in *she*, *shells*, and *shore*. The long *e* sound is repeated in *she* and twice in *sea*. And the *ell* sound is repeated in *sells* and *shells*.

This tongue twister is based on a real person. Mary Anning lived in Great Britain in the 1800s. As a child, she and her brother collected and sold shells to help support their family. They ended up discovering a new kind of dinosaur. And Mary became a successful scientist!

Rocco's stepdad is a sailor.
He tells the class:

"A sailor went to sea, sea, sea
to see what he could see, see, see.
And all that he could see, see, see
was the bottom of the deep blue sea, sea, sea."

This tongue twister provides another example of homophones. *See* and *sea* sound the same but mean different things.

Does the rhythm of all those *see*'s and *sea*'s make you think of ocean waves? It's supposed to!

15

Mimi's mom is a musician.
She tells the class:

"A tutor who tooted a flute
tried to tutor two tooters to toot.
Said the two to the tutor,
'Is it tougher to toot,
or to tutor two tooters to toot?'"

"Well?" Ken asks. "Which is tougher?"

"Too hard to choose," Mimi's mom says.

Here, two sounds are repeated many times. One sound is *t*, a consonant. The other sound is *oo*, a vowel sound, which is spelled in different ways. How many words can you find with that sound?

Does the rhythm of this tongue twister seem familiar? It's a limerick—a funny poem with five lines, a strong beat, and a special rhyming pattern.

After school, Ken sees that his little sister, Patty, has an eyelash on her cheek. "That means you can make a wish," he explains.

Patty claps her hands and says,

"I wish to wish the wish you wish to wish! But if you wish the wish the witch wishes, I won't wish the wish you wish to wish."

18

Here, the tongue twister depends almost entirely on just one word. *Wish* can be a thing (noun). But it can also be an action (verb).

19

Later, Ken sees Mr. Gilbert again.

"What's that smell?" Ken asks, wrinkling his nose.

Mr. Gilbert grins. "My supper, friend!

FRESHLY—FRIED—FLYING—FISH!
FRESHLY FRIED FLYING FISH!"

According to Guinness World Records, the hardest tongue twister in the English language is "The sixth sick sheik's sixth sheep's sick."

A tongue twister might be easy to say, as long as you go slow. But when you try to say it fast, watch out!

It's been a long, strange day. Ken doesn't want any more surprises. He turns on his nightlight.

But his dad is no fan of nightlights. He says to Ken:

"You've no need to light a nightlight on a light night like tonight, for a nightlight's light's a slight light, and tonight's a night that's light."

Ken Chen sighs and says, "All right."

In this tongue twister, how many words rhyme? How many are repeated? Can you spot any words that have more than one meaning?

Stun-Your-Tongue Fun

Gather your friends together, and hold a Twisting Bee! Take turns saying the tongue twisters below, and vote on who did the best. If there's a tie, have the winners face off and say the tongue twister again. You can also use the tongue twisters that appear throughout this book.

unique New York, unique New York, you know you need unique New York

baboon bamboo, baboon bamboo, baboon bamboo, baboon bamboo

many an anemone sees an enemy anemone

Peter Piper picked a peck of pickled peppers.
A peck of pickled peppers Peter Piper picked.
If Peter Piper picked a peck of pickled peppers,
Where's the peck of pickled peppers Peter Piper picked?

CHALLENGE: Try teaming up with one other person and saying the tongue twisters in pairs!

To Learn More

More Books to Read

Agee, Jon. *Orangutan Tongs: Poems to Tangle Your Tongue.* New York: Disney/Hyperion Books, 2009.

Artell, Mike. *Ten-Second Tongue Twisters.* New York: Sterling, 2006.

Brooks, Lou. *Twimericks: The Book of Tongue-Twisting Limericks.* New York: Workman, 2009.

Internet Sites

FactHound offers a safe, fun way to find Internet sites related to this book. All of the sites on FactHound have been researched by our staff.

Here's all you do:
Visit *www.facthound.com*
Type in this code: 9781404862739

Check out projects, games and lots more at **www.capstonekids.com**

Glossary

alliteration—the effect of repeating several words that begin with the same letter or sound

consonant—all the letters of the alphabet except *a, e, i, o, u,* and sometimes *y* (the vowels)

homophone—a word that sounds the same as another but has a different meaning and spelling, such as *blue* and *blew*

phrase—a group of words that are used together

rhyme—to use words that end in the same sounds

rhythm—a regular pattern of beats, like in music

sign language—a way of speaking that uses hand signs instead of spoken words

vowel—the letters *a, e, i, o, u,* and sometimes *y*

Index

Look for all the books in the Ways to Say It series:

She Sells Seashells and Other Tricky Tongue Twisters
Stubborn as a Mule and Other Silly Similes
Talking Turkey and Other Clichés We Say
You're Toast and Other Metaphors We Adore